W9-BRE-463

You are living **your** story.

OWN YOUR STORY: THE INVITATION. Copyright © 2014 by Bock's Office Publishing. All rights reserved. Printed in the United States of America.

All the essays included in this book were previously published as Facebook posts throughout 2014 by Jodee Bock. Graphics are from Facebook and Internet pages. Cover art by Jodee Bock.

ISBN 978-0-9785722-2-8

First edition: December 2014

10 9 8 7 6 5 4 3 2 1

Own Your Story:

The Invitation

Jodee Bock

(&You)

Bock's Office Publishing

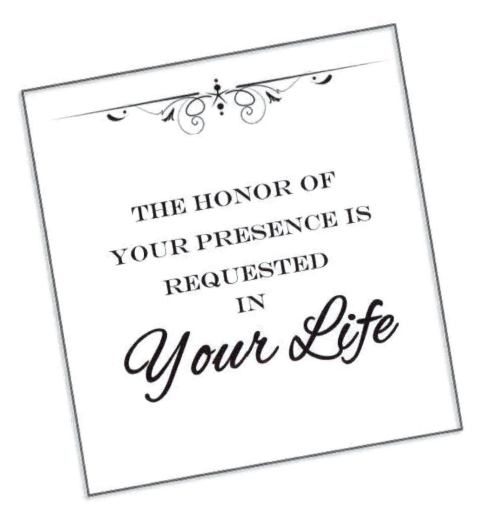

THE HONOR OF
YOUR PRESENCE IS
REQUESTED
IN
Your Life

Welcome!

Have you ever considered the language of an invitation you receive to a wedding or formal event? Traditionally those invitations will request the honor of your presence and often, if you think hard about it, your presence would be the best present you could give.

How do you typically show up to events in your own life? Do you consider the possibility that each day is a brand new present, wrapped up especially for you by the greatest, grandest you you could possibly become? Would that change the story you tell about yourself and your life?

Because every day you are telling that story, not only in the language you use, but also in the way you present yourself and the energy you bring with you. Whether you're aware of that or not, you tend to live into that story.

I've been writing journals and essays since way before I can even remember. One of my majors in college was English with an emphasis on writing, and I set out to make a career of writing early on as a newspaper reporter and editor and later a communications coordinator. Writing is in my blood.

I started blogging before blogging was cool, back in 2004. And then Facebook came into my life, and I turned that writing bug loose on the world through the channel of daily status updates.

That one little idea has become a ritual for me where I take a few moments right away in the morning, and ask what I need to know to begin my day. What I write each day is for me, from wherever those thoughts originate. I'm just grateful that over the years others have begun to appreciate my sharing them through that medium.

"Oh my gosh – you have no idea how perfect that is for me right now!"

"A big thank you – I needed to hear this today!"

"Are you in my head? How do you do that?"

Those comments from others prove that we really are more connected than we are divided. We are much more alike than we are different.

When you discover that every decision you've made has brought you to the exact place you need to be, you start looking at your life differently. Instead of being a victim of your past, you begin to see that all signs are leading to the greatest and grandest version of you: it all depends upon the story you tell. Is it your history/herstory – what really happened – or is it what you say about what happened?

We see our lives through our own eyes, and that perspective shapes our perception.

The ideas in this book will allow you to take a look at the events of your life and make some decisions about the future you choose to live into.

They are pulled from my Facebook status updates and have been lovingly curated by my dear friend Lauri Winterfeldt into loosely themed sections. If you read from the beginning, you may see some themes repeated. After all, there are some lessons I need to learn more than others! ☺

You will find that there are random pages throughout the book that are set up for you to share your own story, thought, idea, or information in order to customize this book for yourself or as a gift to someone else. Wouldn't it be great to receive a book from someone else with the giver's own thoughts interspersed? It's a great way to share a little piece of yourself with someone who means a lot to you.

Another fun way to utilize the book is to think for a moment about a challenge you are facing or an inspiration you are wanting to discover. Open the book and randomly choose one of the entries. More often than not you will find something that will support you or challenge you (in a good way!) right where you are.

I am hopeful that you will choose to accept the invitation this book offers to take a look at the happenings of your life as an observer. The story is yours, and everything you've experienced has brought you to exactly where you find yourself right now – which is exactly where you are supposed to be.

The honor of your presence is requested – by you, to you!

FOREWORD

According to a Buddhist proverb, "When the student is ready, the teacher appears." That was the case in my own life. As I found myself facing an uncertain future, Jodee Bock appeared at a Rotary meeting one day and changed my life forever.

Contained in this book are the first lessons I learned from Jodee and my fellow Master Minders. Over the course of several years, I've learned that what happens to you is less important than what you tell yourself about it. If you tell yourself, "I'm doomed," then you will be. If you tell yourself "I'm powerful," that becomes reality.

In the following pages you'll find concrete ways to make this teaching true in your own life. I encourage you to think deeply as you read and let the words seep into your soul. You are beautiful. You are magnificent. And now you have a powerful teacher to help you realize that, just as she did for me.

Lauri Winterfeldt, Community Education Director
Moorhead, Minnesota Area Public Schools

Your story isn't over yet.

We each have a story we can (and often do) tell about what has happened in our lives that prevents us from being, doing, and having our greatest life possible. You have a story, but you are not that story. Good or bad, right or wrong, you cannot rewrite the beginning of the story … and, unless you're no longer living, the story hasn't ended yet. What would happen if you stopped telling the story about how you can't be, do, or have that great life and picked up the pen and started writing what will become your happy ending? You live into the future you create right now – this minute. What if you could live happily ever after? Here's a secret: YOU CAN! Begin right now to be the hero of your story.

Today notice what the voice in your head is saying to you. And if you're wondering "what voice is she talking about?" that's the one. When you're not aware of what's going on inside your subconscious mind, you will be a prisoner of whatever has been programmed over the years and it will feel like you don't have a choice about who you are becoming. When you begin to notice what seems to just happen to you, you will see that you can reprogram any thoughts or beliefs that aren't serving you in the way you desire. Self-mastery is an inside job and you hold the key!

Do you have any affirmations or mantras you use to start your day? Remember, every morning before your feet hit the floor, you have the power to determine how your day will go, and that is a wonderful time to set your intention. Here is an idea I like to use to start my day (from *A Course in Miracles*):

> **"What would you have me do?**
> **Where would you have me go?**
> **What would you have me say, and to whom?"**

Be open to learning, growing, and sharing each day and you will live an extraordinary life!

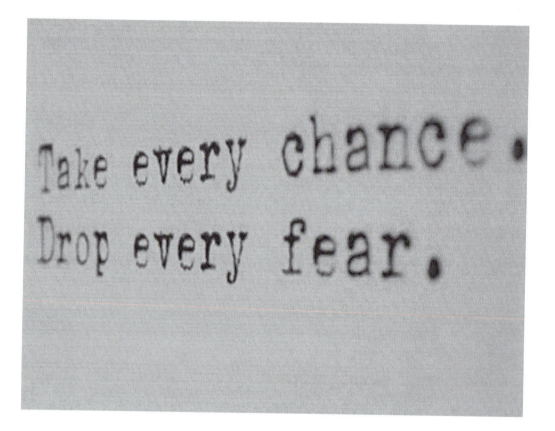

What would you do if you knew you couldn't fail? What keeps you from attempting that? If the answer is fear, just talk yourself through it. What kind of fear? The only fear that's authentic is the fear that threatens your physical survival. Everything else is inauthentic, and gets worse in your mind than it will ever be in reality. Fear is False Evidence Appearing Real. Don't let it get to you. You were meant for greatness and you have a unique ability that will get you there. Stop playing small and get busy on that thing you would do if you knew success was guaranteed. It is! No matter the outcome, you will be even better than you were before – and that's success!

I'm curious why so many people have such difficulty answering the question:

"What do you want?"

Could it be because we've been conditioned not to be selfish? Or that we don't think we deserve whatever it is we might secretly want? Or that we don't think we could have it anyway? OK, so let's say you can't get what you most want. But what if you could? Allow yourself some dreaming and visioning time today. It's OK. You have permission. Now what is possible? Think on that today ... and add "or something greater." Here's a secret: You're never given a dream without also being giving the ability to make it come true. It's the law. What will you do with that?

Many people seem to have been conditioned by the events in their lives not to dream too big because of the possibility of being disappointed. Consequently, they never really experience highs or lows. They've learned to be average. Yes, when you dream big you will experience lows as well. In fact, you learn to welcome them as signals that an up is on the way. What you learn from the mistakes is probably more important than the wave you ride when things go well – although you learn to enjoy that ride, too. A flat roller coaster is a train. Both will get you to your destination … it's your call how you get there.

Your Page

_____

_____

_____

_____

_____

Use your words carefully. Those words create your world. If your thoughts create your reality, imagine what your words do. You can impact the world so much differently by declaring what's right instead of what's wrong. Just for today, look for the ways people in your life are doing things well and point that out. For everything you notice today, choose those words carefully and assume positive intent. I promise you will be grateful and feel wonderfully fulfilled when you go to sleep tonight.

You know all
~~THOSE THINGS~~
you've always
wanted to do?
You should go
DO THEM.

When you stop and think about it, there are very few things about our lives that are not alterable. If you don't like something – nearly anything – about your life, it is possible, then, to change it. There is a distinction, in looking back, between what happened and the story you tell about what happened. In some cases those are two very different perspectives. Your future very likely will become a whole lot like the story you've told yourself about your past until you recognize that. If you don't change direction, you will end up where you are headed. Make the shift today and reap the benefits forever.

It can be difficult sometimes not to take personally what others think or say about you, especially when those opinions are less-than-positive. When you take time to get quiet and really look inside yourself, if you know you've always done the best you could, despite the mistakes and could-have-done-betters, that's really all you have to concern yourself with. Remember: the ego speaks first, and the ego speaks loudest. And often the ego is the scared part of a person. So when others talk about you, it will say more about them than it does about you. Take a risk. Fail forward. Do your best. And let them talk. The doers do and the talkers talk. Learn from your mistakes and continually improve. And never forget: you are awesome!

There is no competition when you are in creation mode because no one else is you. When you put your heart and soul into the achievement or the becoming of something you truly desire, there is no need to compare yourself to others. No one has EVER been exactly where you are and no one else has your unique combination of gifts and talents, so there's really no way to compare anyway. Creation is the ability to begin from nothing, and we've each already done that just by being born our own unique selves. So get into creation mode and forget about being better than anyone else. You're perfect exactly the way you are.

Being aware of your thoughts is so imperative. And noticing when you think thoughts like "I already know this" will help immensely in your ability to be open-minded about learning. Whenever I notice myself thinking "I've heard this before – I already know this," I get out my pen and start taking notes because I know there will be an important message or lesson for me. Remember: you can't change your first thought; you can, however, change every one after that. Be open and aware today and you'll be amazed at how much you will learn!

The Law of Attraction doesn't distinguish between a "good" thought and a "bad" thought; it simply puts in place whatever is your most dominant thought and brings you more of that. So begin to notice the thoughts that automatically flow into your awareness. Are they thoughts of abundance or thoughts of lack? When you realize what you do want, as opposed to what you don't want, make your affirmation one of already having whatever you want or you will continue to receive your thought of wanting, rather than the thought of receiving. If you can see something in your mind, you can hold it in your hand.

Service which is rendered without

joy

helps neither the servant nor the served
But all other pleasures pale into nothingness
before service which is rendered in the
spirit of joy.

-Mohandas Gandhi

How would the results of your actions bring you more joy? Perhaps when you notice that your actions are responsible for your results. If you are seeing the world only through your own eyes, you have probably made up a story to support that point of view. You will be amazed at how everyone around you will get nicer and more supportive when you give up your story about how things are. When you allow awareness to infuse your observations, you will see that as you change your story, you change your experience of the world.

What are the signs in your life telling you? Are you becoming more aware of things that you used to overlook? As we grow in awareness, we will begin waking up to the messages our lives are telling us. Whether it's a song on the radio or a bumper sticker on the car in front of you, begin to notice how everything is lining up for your greatest good. I just turned on the radio to prove my point. Here are the lyrics I heard: "What doesn't kill you makes you stronger." Hmmm ... do you suppose there's a message there for me? I think so. Watch today and just notice what you notice. What is your life telling you?

Socrates was an ancient Greek philosopher who told us, through others' writings, most notably Plato's, that "the unexamined life is not worth living." He believed that everything humans needed to live a full life was experienced through self-discovery. So next time you feel compelled to look outside yourself for answers, or ideas, or solutions, or inspiration, get quiet and look inside. What do you already know that you've forgotten, or covered up, or buried? Tap into your own inner wisdom today by waking up to something that frustrates or upsets you and asking "What is this here to remind (re-*mind*) me?"

"I now *release* the drama of my past. I consciously *create* my future."

Everydayaffirmations.org

There are so many lessons and messages we hear that we really do know – theoretically. It's one thing to know them in our heads … sometimes it's another thing to really internalize them. One of those messages many people have trouble with is not worrying about other peoples' opinions, especially when they are critical or negative. Just remember, things could always be worse – you could be them!

I AM

TWO OF THE MOST
POWERFUL WORDS;
FOR WHAT YOU PUT
AFTER THEM
SHAPES YOUR REALITY.

Affirmations are so powerful, even if you don't fully buy into them at first. In fact, "affirmation" is simply an affirming of what you're saying, thinking, or being. So a subconscious thought like "I'm not good enough" or "I don't deserve it" that runs like a recording through your mind will affirm that thought. As you begin to notice what that voice has been saying, you can change it. You do the affirming instead of allowing it to run rampant and affirm what you don't want. Create your own "I AM" affirmation and consciously live into that.

Oh how much more fun and interesting life is when you give up victim mode! Don't wait for a crisis to change your point of view. Take stock right now and look at the areas of your life that could use a little tweaking. If you're not happy about one of those areas, the people who are with you in that area probably aren't happy either. Stop making excuses and take responsibility for whatever's not working. The day I realized that I was the only thing all my problems had in common was one of the turning points in my life – I just wish I had woken up to that fact sooner. You take care of you and the rest will fall into place.

Most of us, if we're honest, believe that we need to keep our word in every situation. So we play small, because we only take action on what we know we can accomplish. "I gave my word," we think, "and I don't want to fail." There is a distinction between "keeping" your word and "honoring" your word. The difference is intention. What do you really, really want? Make the choice that leads in that direction. Simple, not always easy. But when you know you have done your very best with the information you had at the time, make the call. If you make a mistake, or get new information later, be authentic about where you are and where you were. Honor your word by coming clean with people who need to hear from you. Just don't be paralyzed into inaction because you're afraid you'll make a mistake.

Look at the BLANK PAGES before you with COURAGE

What has your conditioning created inside your mind? When you hear the weather forecast, you hear "20% chance of rain"; I don't think I've ever heard a meteorologist talk about the "80% chance of sun." The first thing we notice is when something's wrong, not when something's right. The attention we give to people, situations, news, is on the negative. Why is that? Today, instead of asking someone "What's wrong?" ask them "What's right and great in your world today?" Be the bringer of positive weather wherever you go. When the possibility exists to look on the bright side – even if it's a slim possibility – go with that instead of where gravity wants to pull you. You will feel better, and so will everyone around you.

Your Page

_____

_____

_____

_____

_____

The really cool thing about building your own awareness is that you have the ability to take 100% responsibility for everything that occurs to you and for you. If you see everything as working together for your good, even if you don't understand why at the time, you will grow exponentially. When you get that it's not about judgment and victim thinking ("why me" turns into "why not me"), you will really get how faith and trust works every single time. I have learned the best lessons when I notice my little voice saying "yeah, but." Everything that comes after that puts me on a higher path, because I see that I've been making excuses and can choose differently. I've learned a lot, too, by asking myself "What keeps happening to me?" When I recognized that in gratitude rather than in victimhood, it changed my life for the better. What's your awareness telling you?

Argue for your limitations and they'll be yours. In fact, argue for anything and the universe will be there to grant your wish. Whenever you feel yourself wanting to defend or debate, just know then is the perfect time to really listen and learn. It may take some time and effort, this paying attention to your feelings, but it's so worth it when you begin to realize that you are responsible for everything that comes into your awareness. The best lessons will be given in times of upset or frustration, so pay attention and ask "What is this here to teach me?"

There is a distinction between what you know and what you believe. Beliefs become truths if you believe them long enough, and they generally are placed there by someone else. Knowingness, however, just is. There is something deep down that, despite what others may say is the truth (usually "their" truth) and that you should believe it, may go against conventional wisdom and feed you from the inside out. When you know something, and you know you know it, there is no going against it – at least not for very long. Search inside yourself for your knowingness and begin to follow that spark. Challenge old beliefs that were placed there long ago and haven't been examined in the light. Be true to your Self and you may find that instead of swimming upstream, you can go with the flow.

Your Page

_____

_____

_____

_____

_____

Have you ever attended a basketball game as a spectator where your viewpoint is from the bleachers? What are you talking about from that perspective? If you're really attentive, you probably notice the good defense, or celebrate a great play. You may yell at the officials, or even the coaches if something happens you don't agree with. Have you ever been on the court in a basketball game? The talk from that perspective is very different. You're helping your teammates know when a screen is being set, or you're calling out the plays. When you're in the stands, at best, the talk is *about* the game. When you're on the court, the talk *is* the game. Translate that to your life. Are you in the stands or on the court of your life? You'll know if you listen to the talk around you. Is it *about* your life or is it *creating* the experience of your life? Get in the game and be present by changing your talk.

Even if your hands are shaking, and your faith is broken. Even as the eyes are closing, do it with a heart wide open.

– Say by John Mayer

Never underestimate the power of a positive word. It's awesome to think positively about someone; it's even better to actually share what you're thinking with that person or those people. And, if you have something to get off your chest, just say it. As glorious as positive feedback is, true and honest concern is just as appreciated when it's shared with love. So, to use the words of singer John Mayer, say what you need to say. Wouldn't it be a fabulous life if we never had to second guess what people are actually thinking and could just go with whatever they say being the truth, the whole truth, and nothing but the truth? It's exhausting to have to wonder.

All of our lives are made up the results of the choices we make. It's never about what happens to us on the outside, it's always about how we react from our emotions or respond from our thinking. Even when things around us seem to be chaotic, there is order in the chaos if you just look for it. "When you're down and out, lift up your head and shout: 'It's gonna be a great day!'" So be it. So it is.

Discovering the answer to the question "What keeps happening to me?" and then getting real about that, will be a huge part of your personal growth journey because it will allow you to realize that whenever you have a problem in your life, you are there for it. In my own life, it turned out that I was the common denominator whenever I got a result I didn't want, whether it was my job(s), my relationships, my hobbies or whatever I was involved with. If something's got to change in your life, take a look in the mirror and know that the person you see there has everything needed to live the life you were born to live. If not now, when?

YOU ARE ALLOWED

You are allowed to have confidence in crazy ideas.
You are allowed to sign your own permission slip.
You are allowed to stop researching & start experimenting.
You are allowed to try things before you fully understand them.
You are allowed to define your own success.
You are allowed to start many things and not finish most of them.
You are allowed to figure out how to do the work without doing the part you don't like.
You are allowed to push your comfort boundaries.
You are allowed to fail. A lot.
You are allowed to push yourself harder than you ever have before.
You are allowed to invent a new way to do it.
You are allowed to make work feel like play.
You are allowed to love what you do & the way you do it.

If you aspire to do great things and make a huge impact in the world, just know that that intention has already set your desire in motion. Just as peace in the world begins with peace in you, so every action you take, no matter how seemingly small, has a ripple effect on the pond that is the world. You, like a teacher, affect eternity because you never know where your influence stops. Do not wait for someday to begin your world-impacting journey. Simply by your being here, it's already started. Be on purpose today.

Your Page

_____

_____

_____

_____

I've always called myself a recovering perfectionist because I am learning that perfection isn't all it's cracked up to be. Looking through the eyes of a perfectionist, I had become much more focused on what's not right with me than what is, even though there are many, many more things that are right. Noticing the language I used – even in my head – has been a big aha, and has allowed me to switch from language like "I can't" to "I choose not to." Really examine your thoughts and your beliefs. Ask yourself "Is that true?" and see how many times you believe thoughts that just aren't true. Your mind is so powerful and awareness will allow you to direct that power toward what you do want and away from what you don't. Whether you think you can or you think you can't, either way you'll be right. Focus on the CANs today!

BELIEVE IN YOURSELF

Trying to be all things to all people discounts the opinions and feelings of the most important person in your life: you. As you become more Self-centered and responsible (able to *respond* as opposed to being stuck in *reaction* mode), you will see that you are also able to listen to others' opinions without taking them on. Of course it is favorable to you to be open-minded and willing to learn. But when others' opinions matter so much to you that you are willing to forego your own wisdom, you are giving your personal power away. Be kind. Be authentic. Be YOU.

Everything that is not green or water was created twice: first in the mind of the creator and then in real life. So imagination is hugely important to cultivate and honor. And creation goes hand-in-hand with destruction: you must destroy silence to create music; you must destroy the blank canvas to create a painting. And you must destroy old ways of being to create new pathways. So don't be afraid to get messy. You need to get beyond your reasons why something won't work in order to get out of your comfort zone into the place where anything is possible. What could you do if you knew you couldn't fail? Create it in your mind so you can hold it in your hand.

I love the quiet of the morning when absolutely anything is possible. We are gifted with a new morning every single day. It's like a do-over every 24 hours. What will you do with this brand new opportunity? Make it an experiment. Set your intention with just a little bit of quiet time in the morning, and then take stock with a little bit of quiet time before you go to sleep. Then, based on what you observe, begin to direct your subconscious mind to work on the details while you sleep. That subconscious mind is like a GPS: it works great when you tell it where you want to go. Until you put in the coordinates, it just sits there, waiting. Be intentional today.

Your Page

_____

_____

_____

_____

_____

Who are you following or looking up to? Who are you allowing to make your decisions for you? When you were a kid, your parents told you that you become who you hang around with and they also told you about the concept of "guilt by association." It's still true. When you allow someone else to dictate your actions and your thoughts, you better make sure that's someone worth following. You will become who you hang out with, so look around. Never let someone else steal your dream. Be aware of your own calling and listen. You already have a future pull inside of you – just like the acorn has the future pull of an oak tree inside of it. If you leave the acorn on the table, it can't achieve its destiny; if you don't put yourself in the place you can succeed, you won't achieve yours either. Give yourself and the world the gift of your best self.

If you were at a buffet and you could eat absolutely anything you saw without gaining any weight or violating any health rules (gluten, vegan, etc.), what would you do? Would you take one of everything and enjoy it? Would you follow the rules anyway (eat veggies before dessert)? That buffet is your life. Where have you put restrictions on what you can be, do, or have? The whole spectrum of experiences is there for your taking, but, if you're like most of us, you've put so many rules on yourself that you can't even see the possibilities. Today ask yourself "why not?" when you notice your old conditioning shutting you down. Did you make a decision many years ago about how you "should" be based on someone else's suggestion or command? Free yourself today from the constraints of your past and choose all over again to expand your awareness. Your life is calling you to LIVE it!

It's great to focus on your strengths, and to put yourself in the place where you can best utilize them for the benefit of the world. It's also great to imagine where you really want to be, and then get real with yourself and see whether or not there are areas you'd like to shore up some growth opportunities. None of us is perfect and there is absolutely no benefit to anyone by attempting to become perfect. However, there are certainly areas in each of our lives where we could become better. If we ignore our blind spots, or deny that we have them, we will lose out on possibilities to better serve ourselves and the world. Focus on your strengths, but leave a little room in your day to become more awake to what you don't even know you don't know.

everything will be okay

in the end.

if it's not okay,

it's not the end.

(unknown)

Please don't let someone else – anyone else – tell you how to live your life. Please pay attention to what makes your spirit soar. That's the only gauge you need. If your feelings produce your actions, and your thoughts creation your feelings, then in order to get different action, you'll need to change your thoughts. And YOU are in charge of your conscious thoughts. Life is a great big series of events, and the more fun and exciting and liberating events you can experience, the more amazing your life will be. Whatever makes you feel good, do more of that!

Your Page

_____

_____

_____

_____

_____

I've heard it said that "Man Plans, God Laughs." I do believe, however, that without a destination in mind, we may wander aimlessly through our lives. So plan your work and work your plan, but don't be so attached to it that you miss the possibilities you might not have thought of. When you set your affirmations, add "this, or something greater" so there is room to allow God to participate. I love the idea of God laughing with me over our success rather than at me for playing way too small.

Stop apologizing for who you are and what you are called to do in the world. You apologize by not stepping into your greatness. You apologize by allowing others who are even more afraid than you to stop you because of a comment they may have made to you (which is more about them than about you anyway). You apologize when you experience the thrill of touching on your purpose and then shutting down because you've been told by someone somewhere in your past that you should put your attention on others' happiness over your own. Your gifts – the amazing, unique abilities given only to you – do not belong to you. You are simply the messenger. Stop ripping the world off by keeping them only to yourself.

Whenever you choose to take action, remember those key words: **You Choose**. Unless you are physically in chains, every action to take – or not take – is ultimately up to you. Many people allow themselves to be imprisoned by their own thoughts and beliefs about how they "have to" do something. We have been gifted with free will, which allows us to choose. We may not like the consequences, but we still have the ability to decide for ourselves. So the next time you hear yourself say something like "I have to go to class" or "I have to make dinner," ask yourself if that's really true. Do you have to? Or do you choose to? Remember: the truth will set you free.

Do you know what it means to be in "flow" state? It's defined as "a feeling of energized focus, full involvement, and enjoyment in the process of the activity. In essence, flow is characterized by complete absorption in what one does" (Wikipedia). I have discovered that when I'm in that state, I feel energized and enlivened ... and at some point my old conditioning kicks in and I stop myself from that feeling because I'm not "supposed" to feel that good. It must be my ego wanting to feel validated, and that can't be a good thing, my conditioning tells me. And that's when I've stopped myself from dreaming big and following where those dreams guide me. Why have I done that? Is it a decision I made a long time ago that no longer serves me? Yes, that's exactly what it is. And I'm able to choose differently now. And I do. And that's the aha. Choose differently now.

I have become super aware of the language I choose when communicating with others because I'm concentrating more on what I'm telling myself first. There is a huge distinction between noticing self-talk and beating said self up with that internal dialogue, and rewarding the discipline that allows the awareness. This retraining of thoughts is a big process, but the results are so worth the effort when you begin to see the distinctions in real life. So today, Notice – Reframe – Speak – Listen – Observe - and Notice. Make it a game. It's so much more fun to be responsible for your own results!

You know the definition of insanity, right? Doing the same thing over and over and expecting different results? If you haven't changed, you haven't learned. Take a look at an area in your life where you might be holding on to an old belief even when it doesn't serve you anymore. Being open-minded really is the first step to realizing that sometimes being right and being accurate aren't the same thing. Don't worry about what other people think – do what makes you feel great. After all, that's the key to living a life you love. What old belief are you willing to give up today?

Your Page

_____

_____

_____

_____

There are many benefits to consciously choosing to achieve or pursue something. Not only do you achieve or acquire the thing you desire, you become a disciplined person in the process. Sometimes that goal-setting process is something we think we *should* do, so the energy we put into that process is reluctant, resentful, and based on the fear we may have if we don't complete it. Instead of "shoulding" all over yourself, what if you imagined how you'd like to feel at the completion of that goal and then just took action that caused that feeling? You would be training your subconscious to pursue that feeling, and almost trick it into the achievement of that goal. Perhaps the biggest benefit of your persistence and deliberation is who you become in the process. So imagine what a person who already is what you're wanting to become would do and just do that. You are SOOO powerful. Step into it!

Through whose eyes
am I seeing this?

Be so strong in your convictions and mindset that nothing – no, not anything – will bring you down. You are in charge of your thinking, and your thinking creates results. When you know how to think, you can have anything you want, whenever you want it. It is possible to live a life of no excuses; you just have to know what you want and then commit to it. When your mind is set on success (the progressive realization of a worthy ideal), it is like a thermostat, and whatever is necessary for achievement of that worthy ideal will show up. Be strong and be of good courage.

I love that Facebook asks the question "What's on your mind?" It's such a great way to begin a conversation. When you really stop and think about it, whatever comes to you in response to that question really is "on your mind." Are you noticing what's wrong and needs to be "fixed"? Or do you see what you appreciate and send a message of thanks? Whatever's on your mind will produce an emotion, which then produces an action, which produces a result. It all starts with what's on your mind. So notice today what's on your mind when you're not noticing. You can't alter what you're not aware of.

What if we all focused just a little more on what's right in our lives today instead of what's wrong? For many of us, it will take some effort because our default – what we are thinking when we're not aware of what we are thinking – is probably not as positive as it would be if we were aware. But the tiny little bit of effort it will take to start turning our collective energy toward the positive is oh so worth it. "What if" is such a powerful phrase when it is used on purpose and toward a desired future, if even for the second it takes to disrupt the pattern. So let's imagine and dream and aspire and stretch our capacity for greatness just a little bit today. Your future thanks you!

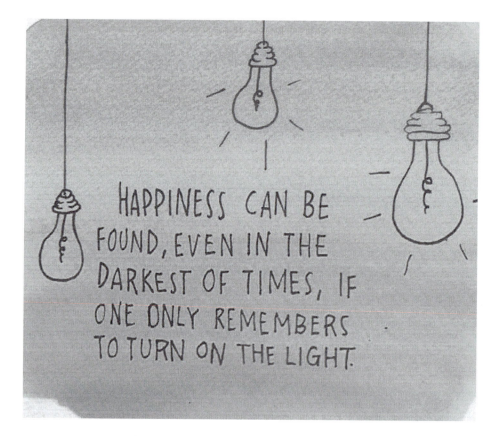

HAPPINESS CAN BE FOUND, EVEN IN THE DARKEST OF TIMES, IF ONE ONLY REMEMBERS TO TURN ON THE LIGHT.

Final Thoughts

This has been such a great project for me because I am beginning to understand more and more that we teach what we most need to learn. Just when I think I might be making some progress in a certain area, I'm given a challenge – and the response or reaction I have to that challenge will let me know whether I need to celebrate or get back to work.

The distinction between information that's there to redirect us, and information there to validate us is the feeling it creates. If you're feeling heavy about the information, it's probably because you still have something to learn or master around that topic. If you're feeling lighter, it's a good bet that you have overcome something that previously might have been a redirection.

Information is fantastic. It shows up in *form* (outside of us) so that we can examine it, process it, deliberate over it, decide about it, and act accordingly upon it (or choose not to).

Inspiration, on the other hand, is internal. It's not so much a doing as it is a feeling. A being. A knowing. For me, inspiration is a barometer to help me determine whether a shift in thinking is needed or whether I'm right where I need to be. The information can show up outside of me; the inspiration allows me to determine what to do with and about the information.

When I really get that it's less about what I do and more about what I be, it turns out I often don't even have to take the action to "make" something happen. It's enough to just get straight in my head what my gut is telling me. Then things just seem to work out.

I know, it sounds odd. But I'm not interested in questioning the Universe.

If you're ready to step into your greatness, consider taking one small step in the direction of your dream. Remember, the Universe will meet you where you are and take you higher.

If not you, then who? If not now, then when?

You're ready. Trust your Self.

Acknowledgements

This book wouldn't be a reality or even possible without the amazing friends I've developed through my daily posts on Facebook. While my thoughts are meant to be a way for me to be accountable to myself, I've been so blessed to hear that others find value in my story. Thank you to everyone who has ever read, liked, or commented on any of my Facebook posts.

And to my dear friend Lauri Winterfeldt – thank you for using your editing talents to help me take these random thoughts from idea to reality. You have continued to inspire me by your willingness to take on the concept of transformation in so many areas of your own life. You are a gift.

And, as in my other books, I really want to thank you, the reader, for making this book relevant. I have written blogs and articles for years and have never known if my thoughts have impacted anyone else. Because you have this book in your hand (in whatever form you are reading it), I know that either someone cared enough about you to give it to you, or you found value in purchasing it for yourself. So thank you, _____ (fill in your name), for considering the thoughts and ideas here as inspiration for you to write and share your own story with others.

About the Author

A connector by nature, Jodee Bock is always looking for patterns to help assimilate and associate things, ideas, and people. She learned to read at age three, so has a wealth of knowledge stuffed into her brain, and is continually seeking ways to put that knowledge into action.

While she has learned active listening skills as a life purpose and career coach, Jodee continues to perfect the skill of using that listening to connect with her own Higher Self through a daily attempt at what could loosely be called "meditation" and is learning to trust her gut.

You can get more information about Jodee at her website, www.bocksoffice.com.

All you need is
20
seconds
of insane courage
— and —
I promise you
something great
will come of it

Benjamin Mee
We Bought a Zoo

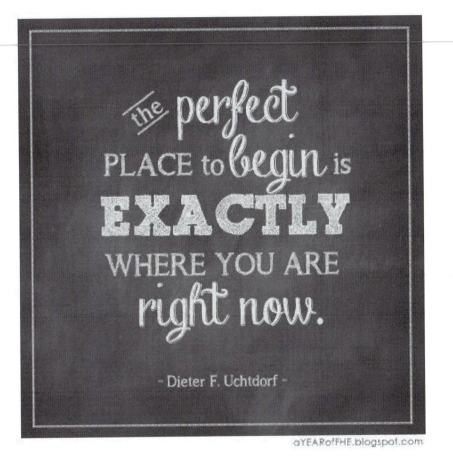

19522980R00051

Made in the USA
San Bernardino, CA
02 March 2015